T0324587

Aalto in Detail

Aalto in Detail

A Catalog of Components

Céline Dietziker
Lukas Gruntz

Birkhäuser
Basel

Keuruu at the Lake "ohra ahonlahti", June 2019

"My name is Aalto, like the architect," he told us in a friendly way. He had caught us while we were sneaking around his apartment building, taking photos of the garage doors. We were in the middle of the National Pensions Institute apartment complex, which the Aaltos built in the early 1950s not far from their own house. This was one of the special encounters that we experienced during our journey through Finland in the summer of 2019, on a hunt for traces of the Aaltos.

"What are you looking for here?" asked Mr. Aalto—who then insisted on showing us his apartment. In this simple two-bedroom worker's apartment, the Aaltos' talent for solving spatial and tectonic problems could be seen and felt. Within a small space, the transition between the kitchen and the dining room was skillfully resolved by means of a pantry with a built-in cupboard. Of course, there had to be a communal sauna in the lower level of the main structure.

After Mr. Aalto dropped off his son at soccer practice, he immediately took us to two unknown houses in nearby Espoo that were built during World War Two—simple, unpretentious wooden houses. On arrival, we started a conversation with one of the owners who invited us on a quick tour through her house. In the detailed design of the stair banisters and the curved wooden ceiling under the roof, the Aaltos' hand was clearly recognizable. This approach is present everywhere in the building: construction problems were handled with a passion and joy for design. Wood was bent. Metal was covered in leather. Glazed ceramic tubes direct light into the depths of the room.

Our extensive catalog of details is the result of this journey, when we visited and documented almost fifty of the Aaltos' buildings from Helsinki, to Jyväskylä, to Turku. Our catalog is not intended to be exhaustive; rather, as a photographic collection, it demonstrates our love of details, which we rediscovered through the work of the Aaltos—Aino (1894–1949), Alvar (1898–1976), and Elissa (1922–1994). This catalog of building elements serves as inspiration for our own architectural work. In a world of digitalized architecture, we should not forget the roots of architectural culture: handcraft.

Céline Dietziker and Lukas Gruntz

Essay

Alvar, 14 years, 1912

"(...) Architecture and its details are in some way all part of biology. Perhaps they are, for instance, like some big salmon or trout. They are not born fully grown; they are not even born in the sea or water where they normally live. They are born hundreds of miles away from their home grounds, where the rivers narrow to tiny streams, in clear rivulets between the fells, in the first drops of water from the melting ice, as remote from their normal life as human emotion and instinct are from our everyday work. Just as it takes time for a speck of fish spawn to mature into a fully-grown fish, so we need time for everything that develops and crystallizes in our world of ideas. Architecture demands even more of this time than other creative work."[1]

Alvar Aalto's essay, "The Trout and the Stream," first appeared in the fall of 1947 with the Italian title, "Architettura e arte concreta," in the architecture and design journal, DOMUS. For this issue, then editor-in-chief Ernesto Nathan Rogers asked his Finnish friend and colleague Aalto to share his thoughts on the relationship between architecture and art. The result is a very personal text. Using compelling metaphors, Aalto recounts his own experiences with architectural projects as well as experiments with wooden furniture designs and sculptural work, which he carried out with his first wife, Aino. In a conversational tone, he describes the Ionic column capital and his love of Italian architectural culture.

Sun terrace, Sanatorium in Paimio (1930s)

He names three "essential" arts—sculpture, painting, and architecture—and discusses how the fields of architecture and abstract art mutually inspire one another. Most significantly, however, he writes about architecture in respect to time, and the importance of having enough of it to be able to develop an architectural idea.

At that point, Alvar Aalto had long been part of the international architectural scene. Within a few years, he had evolved from a young architect influenced by Nordic classicism into a staunch advocate of functionalist modernism. However, the best-known buildings from this early period, the Viipuri Library (1927–35) and the Paimio Sanatorium (1928–33), were already more than a decade old, and in the interim he had become critical of pure functionalism.[2] During this time, his focus shifted to a humanistic architecture that responded to the needs of people and the natural environment. With great sensitivity, he and his first wife Aino put this approach into practice in the Villa Mairea in Noormarkku (1937–39). The town hall in Säynätsalo (1949–52), and Alvar's own experimental summer house built with his second wife, Elissa, in Muuratsalo (1952–54), indicate further moves toward the development of a Finnish regionalism employing traditional materials and historical references.[3]

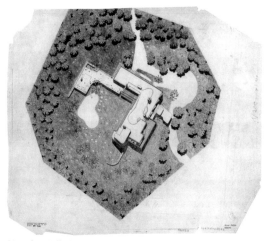

Site plan, Villa Mairea in Noormarkku (1938–39)

These buildings created over a period of three decades are great examples of Aino, Elissa, and Alvar Aalto's openness to current trends, as well as their constant search for distinctive themes. As different as these buildings are, they all exhibit a love of constructive detail. They are based not only on an interest in natural materials and organic forms but also on a general understanding of architecture as a comprehensive design task, first demonstrated by the Defense Corps Building in Jyväskylä (1926–29). The Aaltos' intense engagement with interior design did not emerge until the late 1920s with the winning of the Paimio competition. Due to a lack of commissions during the Great Depression, Aino and Alvar were forced to lay off almost all their staff.[4] Since they scarcely had any other commissions, they put all their time and energy into detailing and designing the interiors and furniture. The result was an impressive total work of art that became a model for their later buildings and design objects.

An organic design concept had already been realized by the Aaltos in Viipuri. Through the circular skylights and undulating ceiling, the natural lighting and acoustics were improved upon, and a more human atmosphere created. Bright colors, often applied in

Steps towards the courtyard, Townhall in Säynätsalo (ca. 1952)

Sample wall, Experimental House in Muuratsalo (1960s)

amorphous figures, and a diverse palette of materials for the building elements served the same ends. Aino and Alvar Aalto's furniture and interior design elements were usually created in conjunction with a building project. In their designs for lighting fixtures, hardware, and glass objects, the same themes and solutions run throughout their careers. Their passion for native wood species was as much a part of this as their eagerness to experiment with a wide variety of construction methods. By using

Entrance side, Defence Corps Building in Jyväskylä (1920s)

Auditorium, Library in Viipuri (1935)

novel methods of bending wood, they were able to produce their cantilever chairs.[5] The transfer of a construction method previously used only for steel tubes to a natural material seems only logical when one considers the Aaltos' careers in retrospect.

Their breakthrough in furniture design came in 1932 with "Number 41," commonly known as the Paimio chair. When the new sanatorium building was completed, enthusiastic articles appeared in several major professional journals. Aino and Alvar Aalto were celebrated as the ideal architect couple and invited to events at home and abroad. Various architecture and design

Wooden mold and vase from the glass series "Savoy", 1936

exhibitions solidified not only their reputation in professional circles but also their fame beyond. Their modern designs and the corresponding production capabilities made it possible to fabricate good, affordable furniture for everyday use. An essential goal and distribution company, Artek, which they cofounded in 1935, played an important role in the emergence of a modern domestic culture in Helsinki and the rest of Finland. The fact that Artek's advertising slogan for quality furniture, "Buy Now Keep Forever," still holds true today speaks for itself.

Much has been written and even more has been speculated about Alvar Aalto's two marriages and his collaborations with his wives. One of the first publications about Alvar Aalto was the —still today—remarkable three-volume edition by Artemis Verlag, published in Zurich in 1963.[6] The introduction to the first volume includes a lengthy, heartfelt note of thanks from Aalto to his current and former collaborators. Along with a brief curriculum vitae, the introduction explicitly states that he ran his office as a

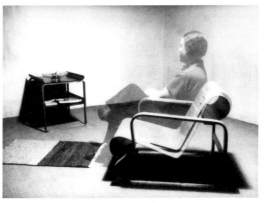

Aino with Paimio-Chair, photographic experiment, ca. 1932

partnership with Aino Aalto from 1924 to 1949, and then with
Elissa Aalto from 1952 onward. This statement is confirmed by the
recollections of numerous employees and further supported
by the repeated observation that Alvar and Aino, and later Elissa,
complemented each other particularly well in the office setting,
both personally and professionally. Despite this, all built projects
continue to be attributed to Alvar Aalto alone. It is astonishing
that, to this day, the achievements of his partners have not been
better researched and appropriately recognized.

The universal interest in the architecture of the three Aaltos
over generations is truly impressive. With their combination of
regional and international elements and use of traditional
building materials, their buildings have even become more con-
temporary. Alvar Aalto himself considered the transition from
a reinforced concrete aesthetic to wood and natural materials to
be the crucial turning point in the development of their architecture.[7] The engagement with established construction methods
and the focus on typically Finnish building materials were prob-
ably the decisive factors behind the authentic uniqueness of their
buildings. Göran Schildt, who was on friendly terms with Alvar
Aalto and wrote several biographies of him, surmised that "the
basic essential of his achievement is that his roots are deep

Elissa and Alvar in the office in Helsinki, 1959

down in the Finnish soil."[8] In an age that is increasingly marked by generic projects, their authenticity is undoubtedly one reason why the buildings of Alvar, Aino, and Elissa Aalto still have such a strong impact.

Alvar Aalto always preferred that people experience his architecture directly rather than just write about his buildings and the ideas behind them.[9] Since he and his partners worked on the designs until the end, often making changes at the last moment on the construction site, this is not surprising.[10] Furthermore, the relationship between inside and outside, which is so typical for them, and the subtle mood of the spaces achieved through direct and indirect lighting can only be perceived on location. The same is true for the colors and the often lighthearted, playful components. Only through close examination does it become clear just how much passion went into the development and execution of every single detail. This is even more impressive in comparison with the situation today, when many architects delegate their responsibility to specialists, which results in a corresponding decrease in architectural quality. That the Aaltos would have handed over control of their designs or the execution of their projects is simply unthinkable.

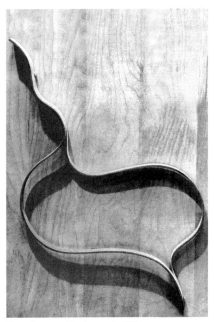

Experiment with plywood, 1934

In his essay mentioned above, Alvar Aalto also describes his preferred way of working. He presents his method of developing
an idea into a project as a meandering, unconscious process that
begins after he has ascertained the essential facts:

"I then move on to a method of working that is very much like abstract art. I simply draw by instinct, not architectural syntheses,
but what are sometimes quite childlike compositions, and in this
way, on an abstract basis, the main idea gradually takes shape,
a kind of universal substance that helps me to bring the numerous contradictory components into harmony." [11]

This almost poetic description corresponds with his comments
about the time factor in creative work. No one would deny that it
takes a lot of time as well as creative space to develop con-
vincing architectural ideas. Talking about the intelligence of the
fingers may sound strange at a time when pencils and sketch

Sketch for Library in Viipuri (1920s)

paper are hardly used anymore and work is increasingly done digitally. By contrast, the topics and projects described here clearly show the opportunities and also the qualities of the analog manner of working.

The built work of Aino, Alvar, and Elissa Aalto is truly multifaceted, joyfully exuberant in design, and at the same time authentic. The Aaltos felt as much responsibility for the context as for the exterior and interior of their buildings. But the strong relationship between the various elements of their architecture is most clearly revealed in their love for the smallest building components—the details.

This catalog demonstrates that these are the very soul of their total works of art. Through intense commitment, careful selection of materials, and use of their own photographs, Céline Dietziker and Lukas Gruntz have thoroughly explored this aspect of the work of the three Aaltos. They deserve full recognition and heartfelt thanks for this valuable, groundbreaking study.

Annette Helle
Zurich, Spring 2022

20

1 Alvar Aalto, "The Trout and the Stream," [1948] in:
G. Schildt, ed., *Alvar Aalto in His Own Words* (Helsinki:
Otava, 1991), 108–9.

2 "Aalto's lifelong attempt to satisfy social and psychological
criteria effectively set him apart from the more dogmatic
Functionalists of the 1920s, whose careers were already
established when he designed his first significant works."
Kenneth Frampton, *Modern Architecture: A Critical History*
(London: Thames and Hudson, 1996), 202.

3 Ibid.

4 Göran Schildt, *Moderna tider. Alvar Aaltos möte med
funktionalismen* (Stockholm: Wahlström & Widstrand,
1985), 85.

5 This new method for manufacturing bentwood was
developed with the help of the Korhonen furniture factory,
and patented in 1933. See exhibition catalog: Enrico Baleri,
Marco Meneguzzo, and Comitato organizzatore salone del
mobile italiano, eds., *Alvar Aalto* (Milan: Cosmit, 1998), 30.

6 Karl Fleig, ed., *Alvar Aalto Band I 1922–62* (Zürich:
Artemis–Verlag für Architektur, 1963), 6–7.

7 Frampton, *Modern Architecture*, 202.

8 Göran Schildt, "Alvar Aalto," in: Fleig, *Alvar Aalto*, 15.

9 Michael Trencher, *The Alvar Aalto Guide* (New York:
Princeton Architectural Press, 1996), 23.

10 Pallasmaa, "From Tectonics," 39.

11 Aalto, "The Trout and the Stream."

Porches

Cultural Centre
Helsinki, Finland
1952–1958

Public Pensions Institute
Helsinki, Finland
1953–1956

Housing Area Sunila Paper Mill
Kotka, Finland
1936–1938, 1947, 1951–1954

Housing Area Sunila Paper Mill
Kotka, Finland
1936–1938, 1947, 1951–1954

Student Union Building
Jyväskylä, Finland
1961–1964

Student Union Building
Jyväskylä, Finland
1961–1964

Architect's House
Helsinki, Finland
1935–1936

Architect's House
Helsinki, Finland
1935–1936

Theatre
Seinäjoki, Finland
1961–1987

Villa Mairea
Noormarkku, Finland
1937–1939

Villa Mairea
Noormarkku, Finland
1937–1939

Lohiluoma Residential Building
Kauttua, Finland
1942

Pedagogical University
Jyväskylä, Finland
1952–1954

Tuberculosis Sanatorium
Paimio, Finland
1929–1933

Tuberculosis Sanatorium
Paimio, Finland
1929–1933

Tuberculosis Sanatorium
Paimio, Finland
1929–1933

Villa Kokkonen
Järvenpää, Finland
1967–1969

Housing Area Sunila Paper Mill
Kotka, Finland
1936–1938, 1947, 1951–1954

Villa Mairea
Noormarkku, Finland
1937–1939

Tuberculosis Sanatorium
Paimio, Finland
1929–1933

Library of the Institute of Technology
Espoo, Finland
1964–1970

Church
Seinäjoki, Finland
1951–1960

Ceilings

University of Jyväskylä Main Building
Jyväskylä, Finland
1954–1956

Church
Seinäjoki, Finland
1951–1960

Concert and Convention Hall
Helsinki, Finland
1967–1971

Cultural Centre
Helsinki, Finland
1952–1958

Maison Louis Carré
Bazoches-sur-Guyonne, France
1956–1959, 1961–1963

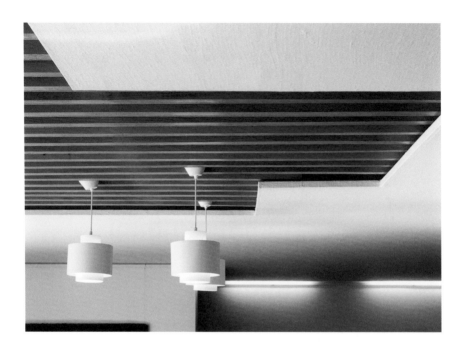

Cultural Centre
Helsinki, Finland
1952–1958

Public Pensions Institute
Helsinki, Finland
1953–1956

Architect's Studio
Helsinki, Finland
1954–1955, 1962–1963

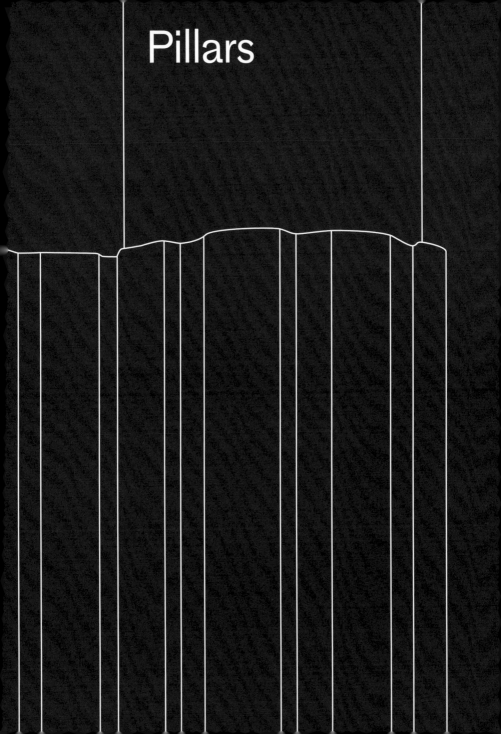

Pillars

Villa Mairea
Noormarkku, Finland
1937–1939

Villa Mairea
Noormarkku, Finland
1937–1939

Enso Gutzeit Housing
Hamina, Finland
1951–1953

Maison Louis Carré
Bazoches-sur-Guyonne, France
1956–1959, 1961–1963

Faculty of Sport and Health
Jyväskylä, Finland
1971

63

Library of the Institute of Technology
Espoo, Finland
1964–1970

University of Jyväskylä Main Building
Jyväskylä, Finland
1954–1956

Theatre
Seinäjoki, Finland
1961–1987

Architect's House
Helsinki, Finland
1935–1936

Main Building of the Institute of Technology
Espoo, Finland
1955–1964

Architect's House
Helsinki, Finland
1935–1936

Concert and Convention Hall
Helsinki, Finland
1967–1975

Public Pensions Institute
Helsinki, Finland
1953–1956

Main Building of the Institute of Technology
Espoo, Finland
1955–1964

Concert and Convention Hall
Helsinki, Finland
1967–1975

73

Administration Building for the City Electic Co.
Helsinki, Finland
1965–1976

Headquarters of Enso-Gutzeit
Helsinki, Finland
1959–1962

Library
Seinäjoki, Finland
1960–1965

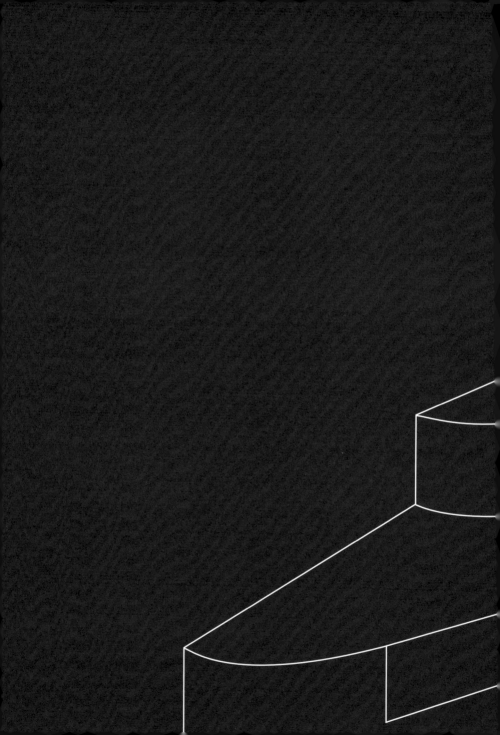

Stairs

Concert and Convention Hall
Helsinki, Finland
1967–1975

Town Hall
Säynätsalo, Finland
1949–1952

Town Hall
Säynätsalo, Finland
1949–1952

Maison Louis Carré
Bazoches-sur-Guyonne, France
1956–1959, 1961–1963

University of Jyväskylä Main Building
Jyväskylä, Finland
1954–1956

Villa Mairea
Noormarkku, Finland
1937–1939

Administration Building for the City Electric Co.
Helsinki, Finland
1965–1976

Rautatalo Office Building
Helsinki, Finland
1951–1955

Public Pensions Institute
Helsinki, Finland
1953–1956

Architect's House
Helsinki, Finland
1935–1936

Architect's Studio
Helsinki, Finland
1954–1955, 1962–1963

Architect's House
Helsinki, Finland
1935–1936

Public Pensions Institute
Helsinki, Finland
1953–1956

Main Building of the Institute of Technology
Espoo, Finland
1955–1964

Library of the Institute of Technology
Espoo, Finland
1964–1970

University of Jyväskylä Main Building
Jyväskylä, Finland
1954–1956

Town Hall
Säynätsalo, Finland
1949–1952

University of Jyväskylä Main Building
Jyväskylä, Finland
1954–1956

Pedagogical University
Jyväskylä, Finland
1952–1954

Library
Seinäjoki, Finland
1960–1965

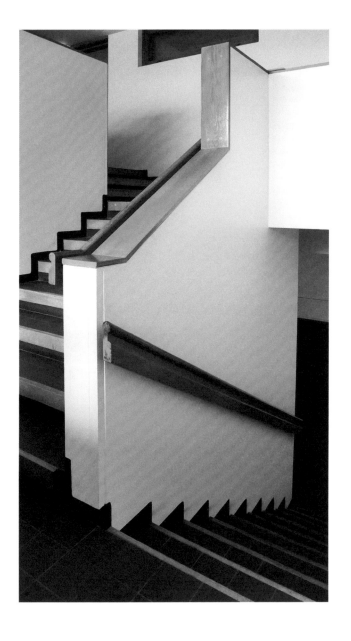

Church
Seinäjoki, Finland
1951–1960

Tuberculosis Sanatorium
Paimio, Finland
1929–1933

Tuberculosis Sanatorium
Paimio, Finland
1929–1933

Turun Sanomat Newspaper Office
Turku, Finland
1928–1929

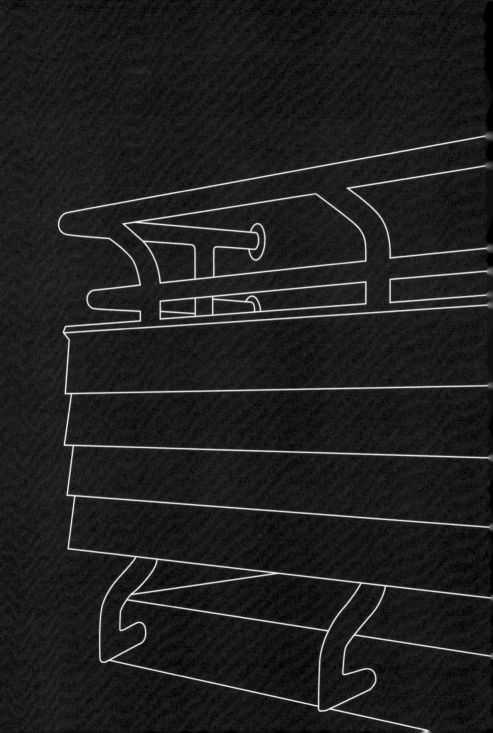

Balconies

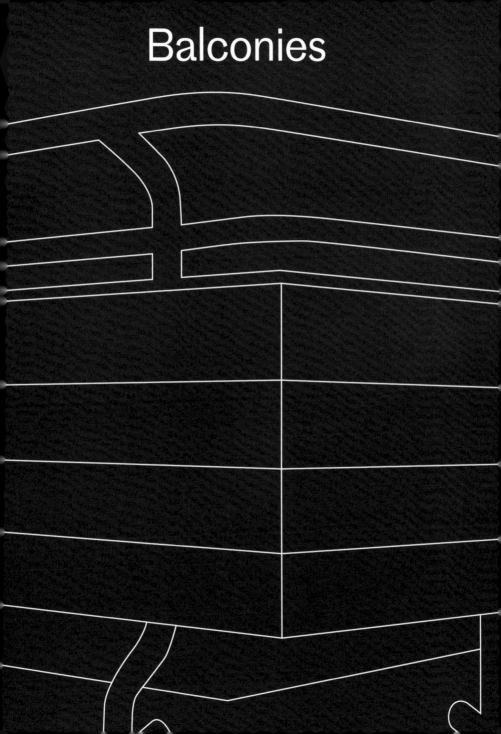

Housing Area Sunila Paper Mill
Kotka, Finland
1936–1938, 1947, 1951–1954

Housing Area Sunila Paper Mill
Kotka, Finland
1936–1938, 1947, 1951–1954

Housing Area Sunila Paper Mill
Kotka, Finland
1936–1938, 1947, 1951–1954

Housing Area Sunila Paper Mill
Kotka, Finland
1936–1938, 1947, 1951–1954

Tuberculosis Sanatorium
Paimio, Finland
1929–1933

Aira Building
Jyväskylä, Finland
1924–1926

Tuberculosis Sanatorium
Paimio, Finland
1929–1933

Tuberculosis Sanatorium
Paimio, Finland
1929–1933

112

Villa Mairea
Noormarkku, Finland
1937–1939

Housing for the Personnel of the Public Pensions Institute
Helsinki, Finland
1952–1954

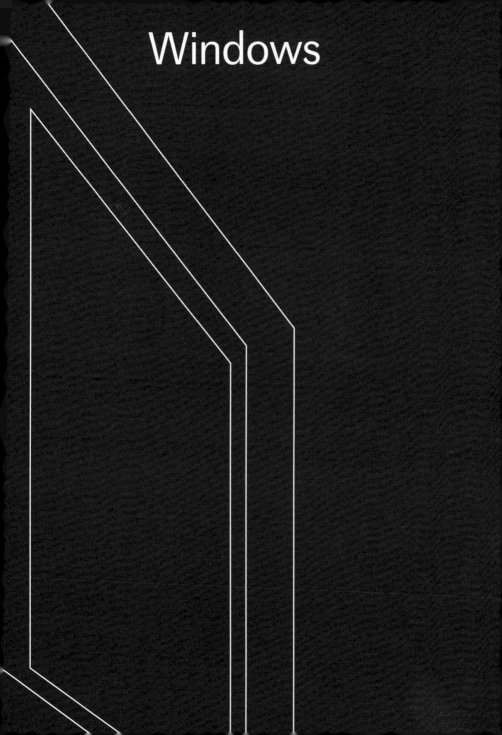

Windows

Town Hall
Säynätsalo, Finland
1949–1952

Summer House
Muuratsalo, Finland
1952–1954

Architect's Studio
Helsinki, Finland
1954–1955, 1962–1963

Farmers Co-operative Building
Turku, Finland
1927–1928

Headquarters of Enso-Gutzeit
Helsinki, Finland
1959–1962

Administration Building for the City Electric Co.
Helsinki, Finland
1965–1976

Rautatalo Office Building
Helsinki, Finland
1951–1955

Administration Building of the Scandinavian Bank
Helsinki, Finland
1960–1965

Housing for the Personnel of the Public Pensions Institute
Helsinki, Finland
1952–1954

Harjuviita Apartment Houses
Espoo, Finland
1962–1964

Town Hall
Säynätsalo, Finland
1949–1952

Town Hall
Säynätsalo, Finland
1949–1952

Tuberculosis Sanatorium
Paimio, Finland
1929–1933

Tuberculosis Sanatorium
Paimio, Finland
1929–1933

Student Union Building
Jyväskylä, Finland
1961–1964

Summer House
Muuratsalo, Finland
1952–1954

Terrace Housing
Kauttua, Finland
1937–1938

133

Terrace Housing
Kauttua, Finland
1937–1938

Tuberculosis Sanatorium
Paimio, Finland
1929–1933

Tuberculosis Sanatorium
Paimio, Finland
1929–1933

Architect's Studio
Helsinki, Finland
1935–1936

Villa Kokkonen
Järvenpää, Finland
1967–1969

Villa Skeppet / Villa Schildt
Tammisaari, Finland
1969–1970

Maison Louis Carré
Bazoches-sur-Guyonne, France
1956–1959, 1961–1963

Building of the Association of Finnish Engineers
Helsinki, Finland
1948–1952

Main Building of the Institute of Technology
Espoo, Finland
1955–1964

Town Hall
Säynätsalo, Finland
1949–1952

Student Union Building
Jyväskylä, Finland
1961–1964

Town Hall
Säynätsalo, Finland
1949–1952

Town Hall
Säynätsalo, Finland
1949–1952

Cultural Centre
Helsinki, Finland
1952–1958

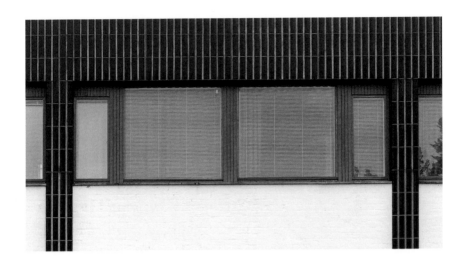

Library
Seinäjoki, Finland
1960–1965

Main Building of the Institute of Technology
Espoo, Finland
1955–1964

Tuberculosis Sanatorium
Paimio, Finland
1929–1933

Architect's Studio
Helsinki, Finland
1954–1955, 1962–1963

Architect's Studio
Helsinki, Finland
1954–1955, 1962–1963

152

Theatre
Jyväskylä, Finland
1964–1982

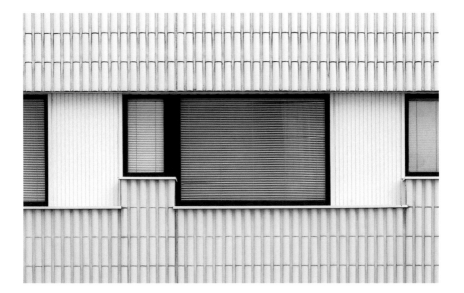

Theatre
Seinäjoki, Finland
1964–1968

Town Hall
Säynätsalo, Finland
1949–1952

Town Hall
Säynätsalo, Finland
1949–1952

Architect's Studio
Helsinki, Finland
1935–1936

Architect's Studio
Helsinki, Finland
1935–1936

Architect's Studio
Helsinki, Finland
1954–1955, 1962–1963

Architect's Studio
Helsinki, Finland
1954–1955, 1962–1963

Architect's Studio
Helsinki, Finland
1954–1955, 1962–1963

Villa Mairea
Noormarkku, Finland
1937–1939

Maison Louis Carré
Bazoches-sur-Guyonne, France
1956–1959, 1961–1963

Maison Louis Carré
Bazoches-sur-Guyonne, France
1956–1959, 1961–1963

Church
Seinäjoki, Finland
1951–1960

Library
Seinäjoki, Finland
1960–1965

Architect's Studio
Helsinki, Finland
1935–1936

Maison Louis Carré
Bazoches-sur-Guyonne, France
1956–1959, 1961–1963

Theatre
Jyväskylä, Finland
1964–1982

Theatre
Seinäjoki, Finland
1964–1968

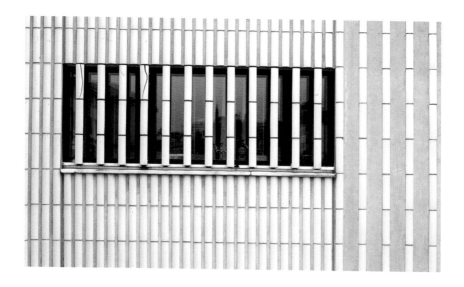

Theatre
Jyväskylä, Finland
1964–1982

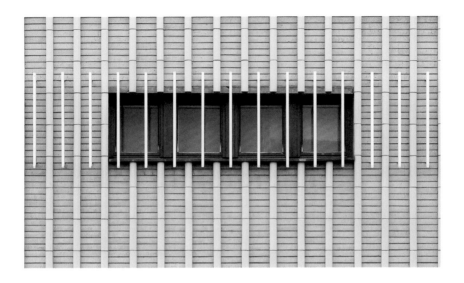

Alvar Aalto Museum
Jyväskylä, Finland
1971–1973

Town Hall
Seinäjoki, Finland
1958–1960

Main Building of the Institute of Technology
Espoo, Finland
1955–1964

Student Union Building
Jyväskylä, Finland
1961–1964

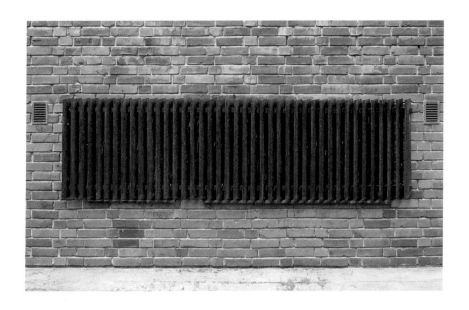

Town Hall
Säynätsalo, Finland
1949–1952

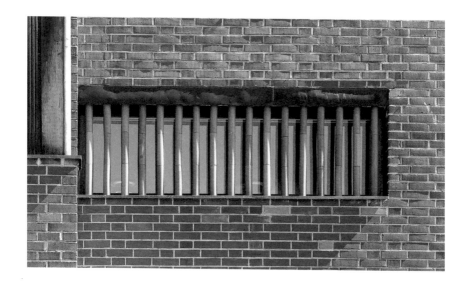

Harjuviita Apartment Houses
Espoo, Finland
1964–1970

Town Hall
Säynätsalo, Finland
1949–1952

Town Hall
Säynätsalo, Finland
1949–1952

Town Hall
Säynätsalo, Finland
1949–1952

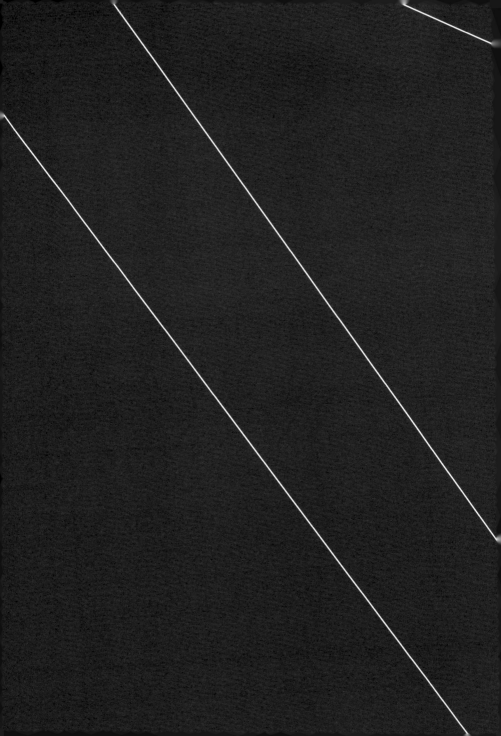

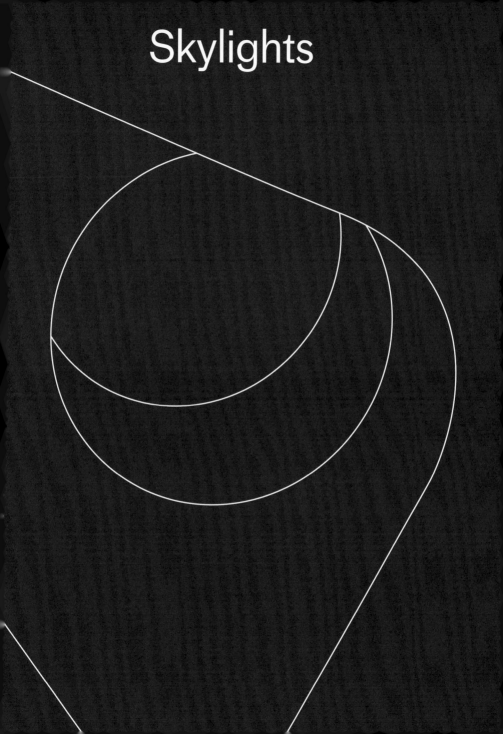

Student Union Building
Jyväskylä, Finland
1961–1964

Headquarters of Enso-Gutzeit
Helsinki, Finland
1959–1962

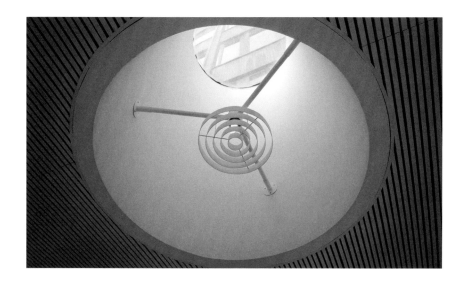

Administration Building of the Scandinavian Bank
Helsinki, Finland
1960–1965

Library of the Institute of Technology
Espoo, Finland
1964–1970

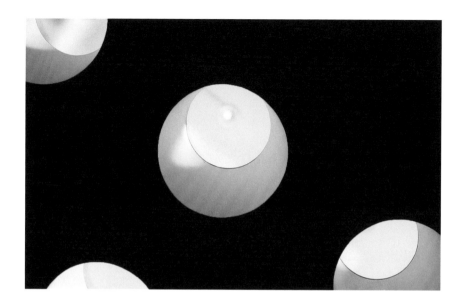

Rautatalo Office Building
Helsinki, Finland
1951–1955

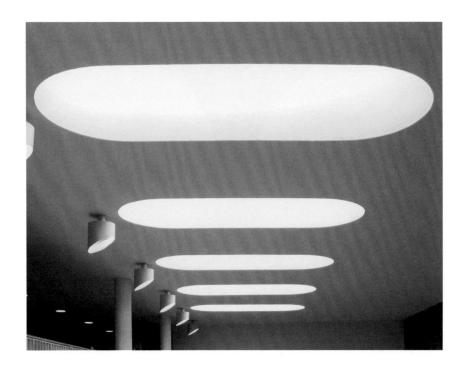

University of Jyväskylä Main Building
Jyväskylä, Finland
1954–1956

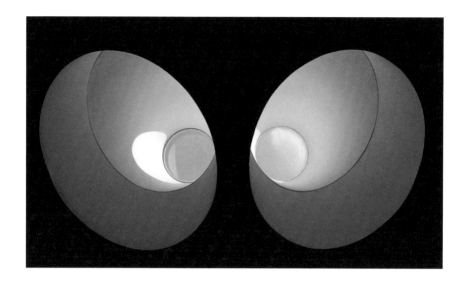

Public Pensions Institute
Helsinki, Finland
1953–1956

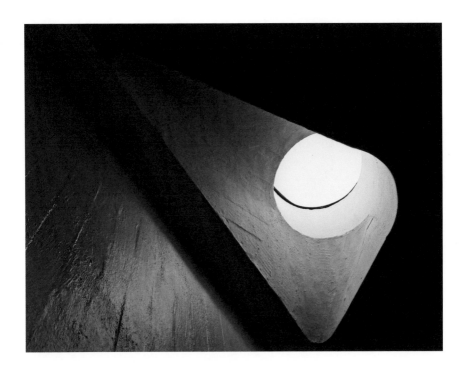

Architect's Studio
Helsinki, Finland
1954–1955, 1962–1963

Administration Building for the City Electric Co.
Helsinki, Finland
1965–1976

Public Pensions Institute
Helsinki, Finland
1953–1956

Academic Bookshop
Helsinki, Finland
1961–1969

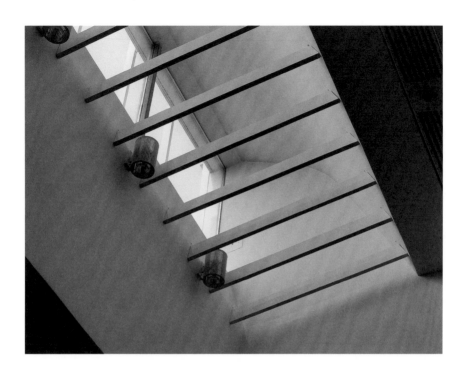

Church
Lahti, Finland
1969–1979

Architect's Studio
Helsinki, Finland
1954–1955, 1962–1963

Architect's Studio
Helsinki, Finland
1954–1955, 1962–1963

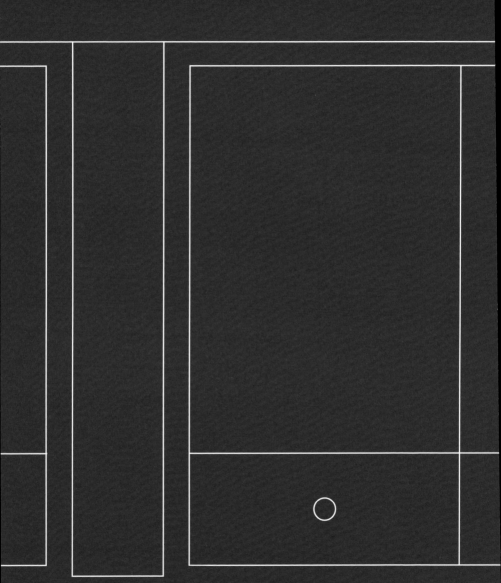

Garage Doors

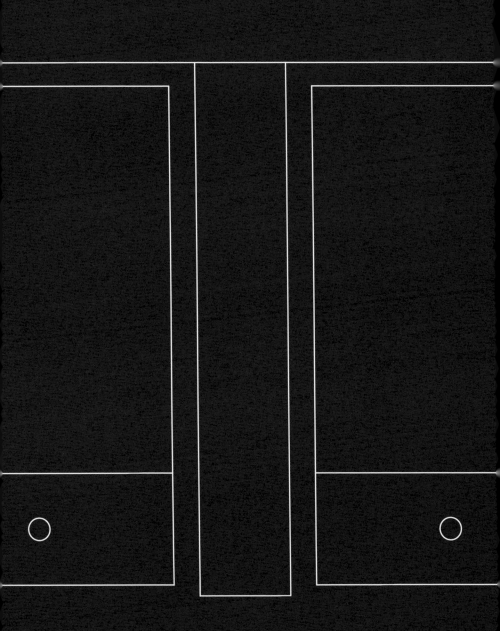

Summer House
Muuratsalo, Finland
1952–1954

Library
Seinäjoki, Finland
1960–1965

Architect's Studio
Helsinki, Finland
1954–1955, 1962–1963

Architect's House
Helsinki, Finland
1935–1936

Alvar Aalto Museum
Jyväskylä, Finland
1971–1973

Villa Kokkonen
Järvenpää, Finland
1967–1969

Enso Gutzeit Housing
Hamina, Finland
1951–1953, 1970–1972

Housing Area Sunila Paper Mill
Kotka, Finland
1936–1938, 1947, 1951–1954

Headquarters of Enso-Gutzeit
Helsinki, Finland
1959–1962

Housing for the Personnel of the Public Pensions Institute
Helsinki, Finland
1952–1954

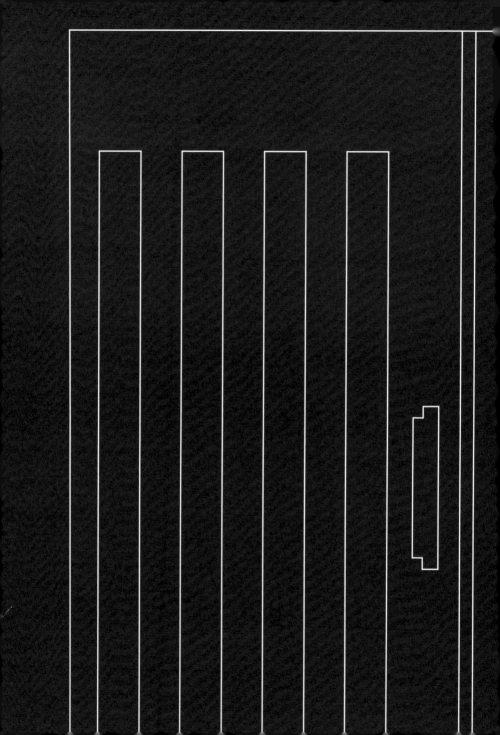

Exterior Doors

Church
Seinäjoki, Finland
1951–1960

Architect's Studio
Helsinki, Finland
1954–1955, 1962–1963

Architect's Studio
Helsinki, Finland
1954–1955, 1962–1963

Architect's House
Helsinki, Finland
1935–1936

Architect's House
Helsinki, Finland
1935–1936

Architect's House
Helsinki, Finland
1935–1936

Enso Gutzeit Housing
Hamina, Finland
1951–1953, 1970–1972

Harjuviita Apartment Houses
Espoo, Finland
1962–1964

Church
Seinäjoki, Finland
1951–1960

Enso Gutzeit Housing
Hamina, Finland
1951–1953, 1970–1972

Student Union Building
Jyväskylä, Finland
1961–1964

Main Building of the Institute of Technology
Espoo, Finland
1955–1964

Summer House
Muuratsalo, Finland
1952–1954

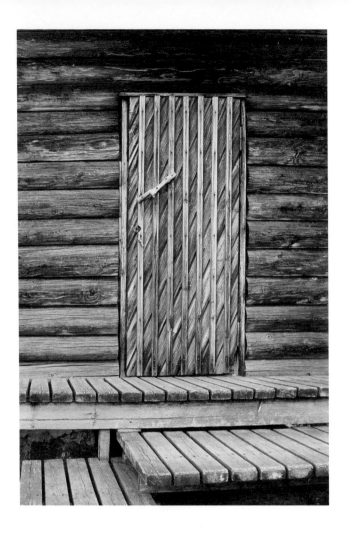

Summer House
Muuratsalo, Finland
1952–1954

Villa Mairea
Noormarkku, Finland
1937–1939

Maison Louis Carré
Bazoches-sur-Guyonne, France
1956–1959, 1961–1963

Sauna and Laundry
Kauttua, Finland
1940–1941

Sauna and Laundry
Kauttua, Finland
1940–1941

Defence Corps Building
Seinäjoki, Finland
1924–1926

Villa Mairea
Noormarkku, Finland
1937–1939

Administration Building for the City Electric Co.
Helsinki, Finland
1965–1976

Public Pensions Institute
Helsinki, Finland
1953–1956

Church
Lahti, Finland
1969–1979

Workers Club
Jyväskylä, Finland
1924–1925

Church
Seinäjoki, Finland
1951–1960

Alvar Aalto Museum
Jyväskylä, Finland
1971–1973

Church
Seinäjoki, Finland
1951–1960

Church
Seinäjoki, Finland
1951–1960

Housing for the Personnel of the Public Pensions Institute
Helsinki, Finland
1952–1954

Housing for the Personnel of the Public Pensions Institute
Helsinki, Finland
1952–1954

Main Building of the Institute of Technology
Espoo, Finland
1955–1964

Cultural Centre
Helsinki, Finland
1952–1958

Harjuviita Apartment Houses
Espoo, Finland
1962–1964

Villa Kokkonen
Järvenpää, Finland
1967–1969

Housing Area Sunila Paper Mill
Kotka, Finland
1936–1938, 1947, 1951–1954

Housing Area Sunila Paper Mill
Kotka, Finland
1936–1938, 1947, 1951–1954

Enso Gutzeit Housing
Hamina, Finland
1951–1953, 1970–1972

Town Hall
Säynätsalo, Finland
1949–1952

Student Union Building
Jyväskylä, Finland
1961–1964

Summer House
Muuratsalo, Finland
1952–1954

Church
Seinäjoki, Finland
1951–1960

Villa Schildt (Villa Skeppet)
Tammisaari, Finland
1969–1970

Defence Corps Building
Seinäjoki, Finland
1924–1926

Farmers Co-operative Building
Turku, Finland
1927–1928

University of Jyväskylä Main Building
Jyväskylä, Finland
1954–1956

Central Finnish Museum
Jyväskylä, Finland
1956–1961

Standard Apartment Building
Turku, Finland
1927–1928

Standard Apartment Building
Turku, Finland
1927–1928

Interior Doors

Rautatalo Office Building
Helsinki, Finland
1951–1955

Public Pensions Institute
Helsinki, Finland
1953–1956

Main Building of the Institute of Technology
Espoo, Finland
1955–1964

Maison Louis Carré
Bazoches-sur-Guyonne, France
1956–1959, 1961–1963

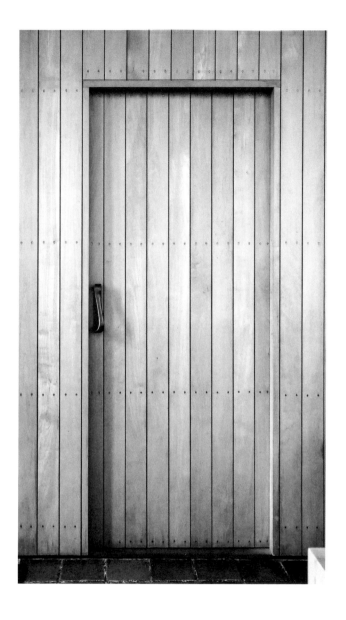

Church
Seinäjoki, Finland
1951–1960

Maison Louis Carré
Bazoches-sur-Guyonne, France
1956–1959, 1961–1963

Town Hall
Säynätsalo, Finland
1949–1952

Maison Louis Carré
Bazoches-sur-Guyonne, France
1956–1959, 1961–1963

University of Jyväskylä Main Building
Jyväskylä, Finland
1954–1956

Housing for the Personnel of the Public Pensions Institute
Helsinki, Finland
1951–1953, 1970–1972

Theatre
Seinäjoki, Finland
1961–1987

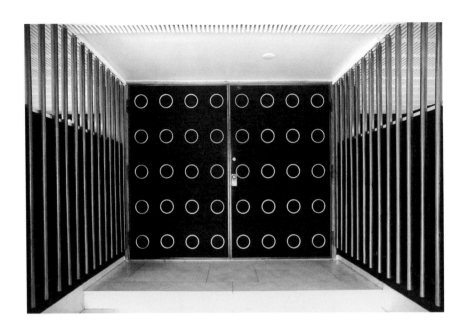

University of Jyväskylä Main Building
Jyväskylä, Finland
1954–1956

Main Building of the Institute of Technology
Espoo, Finland
1955–1964

Faculty of Sport and Health
Jyväskylä, Finland
1971

Tuberculosis Sanatorium
Paimio, Finland
1929–1933

Library of the Institute of Technology
Espoo, Finland
1964–1970

Church
Lahti, Finland
1969–1979

Main Building of the Institute of Technology
Espoo, Finland
1955–1964

Main Building of the Institute of Technology
Espoo, Finland
1955–1964

Church
Seinäjoki, Finland
1951–1960

Main Building of the Institute of Technology
Espoo, Finland
1955–1964

Church
Seinäjoki, Finland
1951–1960

Town Hall
Seinäjoki, Finland
1958–1960

Town Hall
Säynätsalo, Finland
1949–1952

Lift Doors

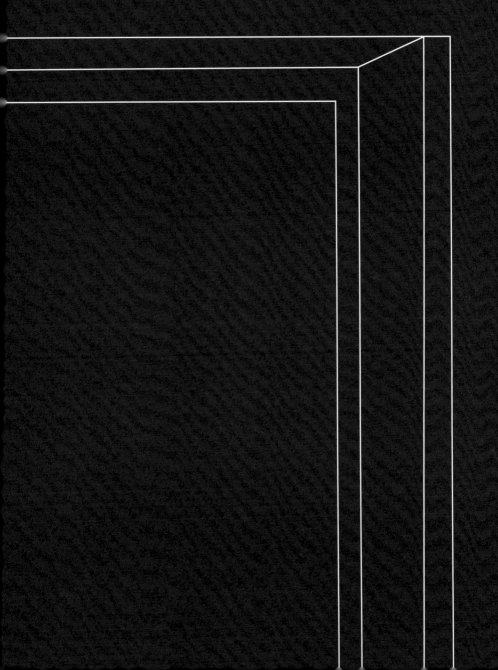

Rautatalo Office Building
Helsinki, Finland
1951–1955

Public Pensions Institute
Helsinki, Finland
1953–1956

Church
Lahti, Finland
1969–7199

Academic Bookshop
Helsinki, Finland
1961–1969

Administration Building for the City Electric Co.
Helsinki, Finland
1965–1976

Rautatalo Office Building
Helsinki, Finland
1951–1955

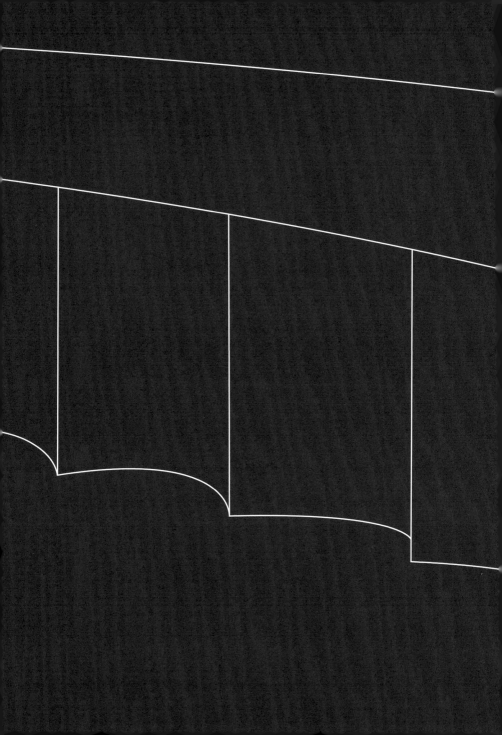

Socle

Summer House
Muuratsalo, Finland
1952–1954

Architect's Studio
Helsinki, Finland
1954–1955, 1962–1963

Aira Building
Jyväskylä, Finland
1924–1926

Defence Corps Building
Seinäjoki, Finland
1924–1926

Cultural Centre
Helsinki, Finland
1952–1958

Villa Mairea
Noormarkku, Finland
1937–1939

Church
Lahti, Finland
1969–1979

Villa Kokkonen
Järvenpää, Finland
1967–1969

Student Union Building
Jyväskylä, Finland
1961–1964

Alvar Aalto Museum
Jyväskylä, Finland
1971–1973

Housing
Espoo, Finland
1940

Church
Muurame, Finland
1926–1929

Public Pensions Institute
Helsinki, Finland
1953–1956

Main Building of the Institute of Technology
Espoo, Finland
1955–1964

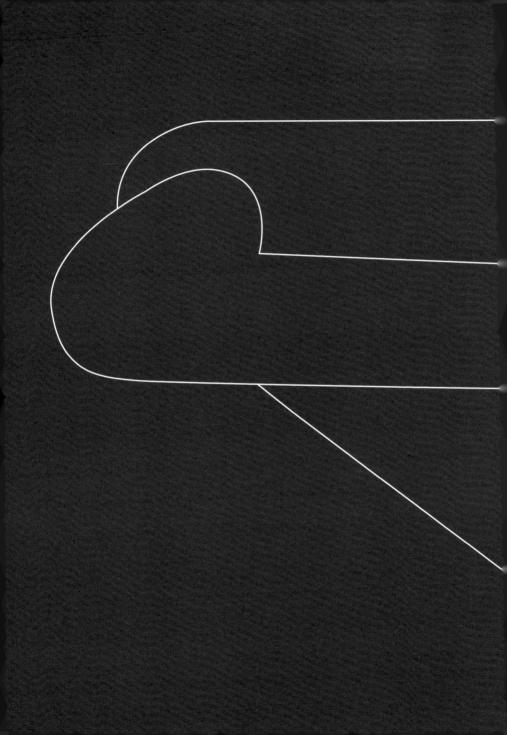

Door Handles

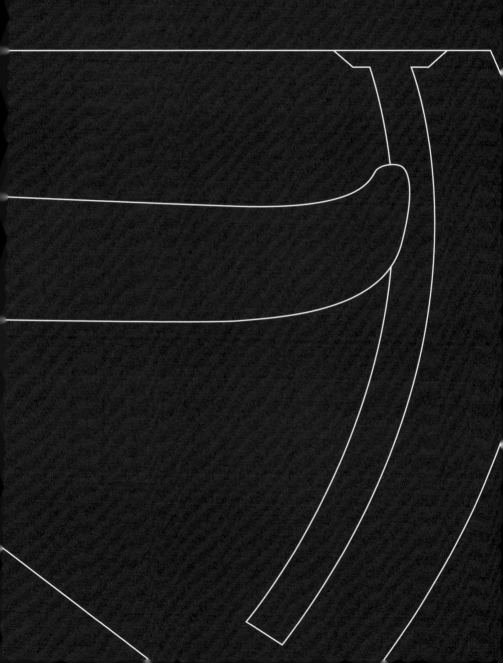

Sauna and Laundry
Kauttua, Finland
1940–1941

Student Union Building
Jyväskylä, Finland
1961–1964

Housing for the Personnel of the Public Pensions Institute
Helsinki, Finland
1952–1954

Cultural Centre
Helsinki, Finland
1952–1958

Public Pensions Institute
Helsinki, Finland
1953–1956

Faculty of Sport and Health
Jyväskylä, Finland
1971

Maison Louis Carré
Bazoches-sur-Guyonne, France
1956–1959, 1961–1963

Viitatorni Highrise Apartment House
Jyväskylä, Finland
1960–1961

Town Hall
Säynätsalo, Finland
1949–1952

Villa Mairea
Noormarkku, Finland
1937–1939

Town Hall
Säynätsalo, Finland
1949–1952

Housing for the Personnel of the Public Pensions Institute
Helsinki, Finland
1952–1954

Headquarters of Enso-Gutzeit
Helsinki, Finland
1959–1962

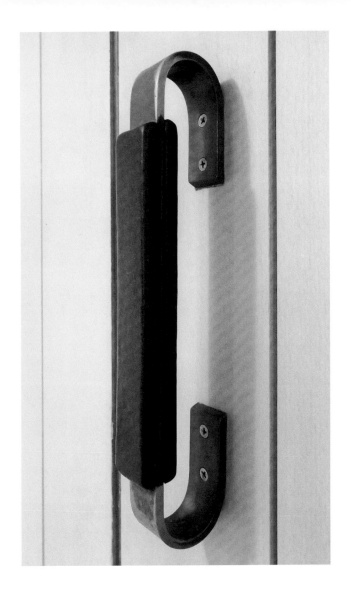

Concert and Convention Hall
Helsinki, Finland
1967–1975

324

Public Pensions Institute
Helsinki, Finland
1953–1956

325

Workers Club
Jyväskylä, Finland
1924–1925

Farmers Co-operative Building
Turku, Finland
1927–1928

Defence Corps Building
Seinäjoki, Finland
1924–1926

Villa Mairea
Noormarkku, Finland
1937–1939

Villa Mairea
Noormarkku, Finland
1937–1939

Architect's Studio
Helsinki, Finland
1954–1955, 1962–1963

Villa Mairea
Noormarkku, Finland
1937–1939

Architect's House
Helsinki, Finland
1935–1936

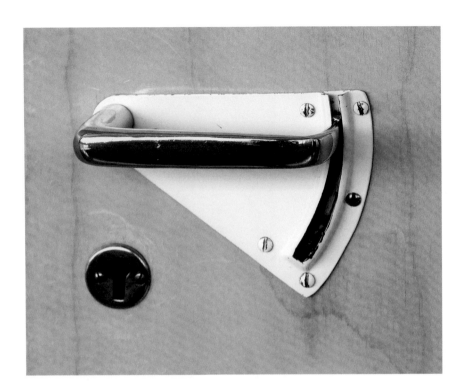

Tuberculosis Sanatorium
Paimio, Finland
1929–1933

Concert and Convention Hall
Helsinki, Finland
1967–1975

Church
Lahti, Finland
1969–1979

Church
Lahti, Finland
1969–1979

337

Academic Bookshop
Helsinki, Finland
1961–1969

Handrails

Main Building of the Institute of Technology
Espoo, Finland
1955–1964

Main Building of the Institute of Technology
Espoo, Finland
1955–1964

Town Hall
Säynätsalo, Finland
1949–1952

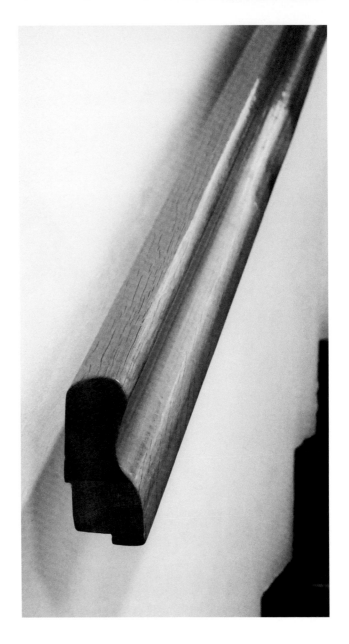

Library
Seinäjoki, Finland
1960–1965

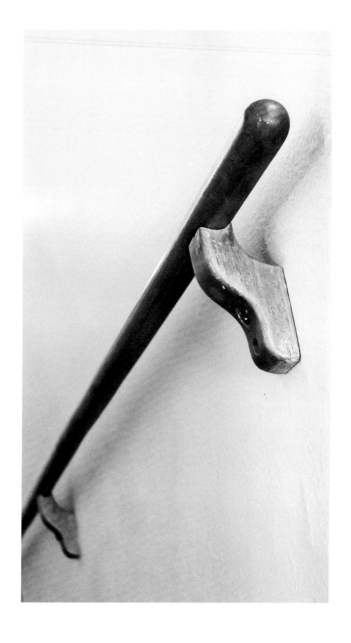

Architect's House
Helsinki, Finland
1935–1936

Town Hall
Seinäjoki, Finland
1958–1960

University of Jyväskylä Main Building
Jyväskylä, Finland
1954–1956

Maison Louis Carré
Bazoches-sur-Guyonne, France
1956–1959, 1961–1963

Pedagogical University
Jyväskylä, Finland
1952–1954

349

University of Jyväskylä Main Building
Jyväskylä, Finland
1954–1956

Administration Building of the Scandinavian Bank
Helsinki, Finland
1960–1965

Main Building of the Institute of Technology
Espoo, Finland
1955–1964

Main Building of the Institute of Technology
Espoo, Finland
1955–1964

Main Building of the Institute of Technology
Espoo, Finland
1955–1964

University of Jyväskylä Main Building
Jyväskylä, Finland
1954–1956

University of Jyväskylä Main Building
Jyväskylä, Finland
1954–1956

Concert and Convention Hall
Helsinki, Finland
1967–1975

Church
Seinäjoki, Finland
1951–1960

Architect's Studio
Helsinki, Finland
1954–1955, 1962–1963

University of Jyväskylä Main Building
Jyväskylä, Finland
1954–1956

Academic Bookshop
Helsinki, Finland
1961–1969

Alvar Aalto Museum
Jyväskylä, Finland
1971–1973

Theatre
Seinäjoki, Finland
1961–1987

Administration Building for the City Electric Co.
Helsinki, Finland
1965–1976

Turun Sanomat Newspaper Office
Turku, Finland
1928–1929

Tuberculosis Sanatorium
Paimio, Finland
1929–1933

Tuberculosis Sanatorium
Paimio, Finland
1929–1933

Turun Sanomat Newspaper Office
Turku, Finland
1928–1929

Cultural Centre
Helsinki, Finland
1952–1958

Theatre
Jyväskylä, Finland
1964–1982

Concert and Convention Hall
Helsinki, Finland
1967–1975

Concert and Convention Hall
Helsinki, Finland
1967–1975

Railings

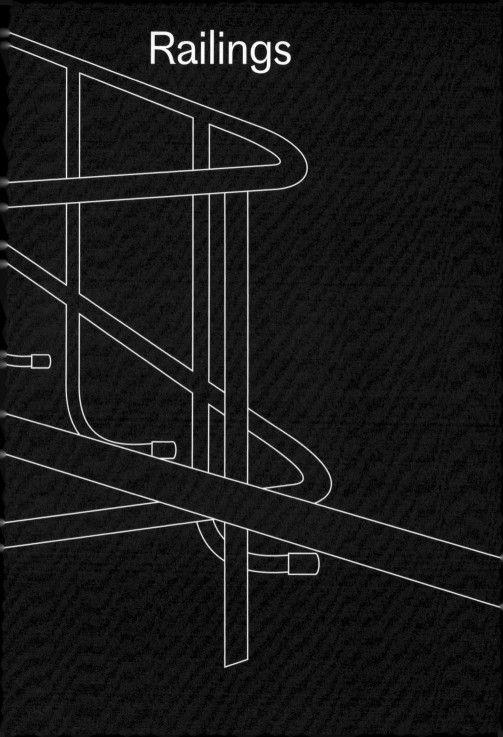

University of Jyväskylä Main Building
Jyväskylä, Finland
1954–1956

Pedagogical University
Jyväskylä, Finland
1952–1954

Main Building of the Institute of Technology
Espoo, Finland
1955–1964

Church
Lahti, Finland
1969–1979

Maison Louis Carré
Bazoches-sur-Guyonne, France
1956–1959, 1961–1963

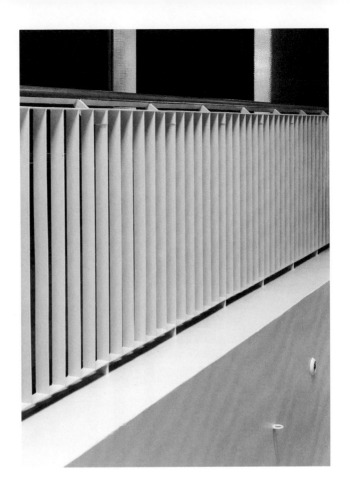

University of Jyväskylä Main Building
Jyväskylä, Finland
1954–1956

Town Hall
Seinäjoki, Finland
1958–1960

Pedagogical University
Jyväskylä, Finland
1952–1954

Library
Seinäjoki, Finland
1960–1965

Tuberculosis Sanatorium
Paimio, Finland
1929–1933

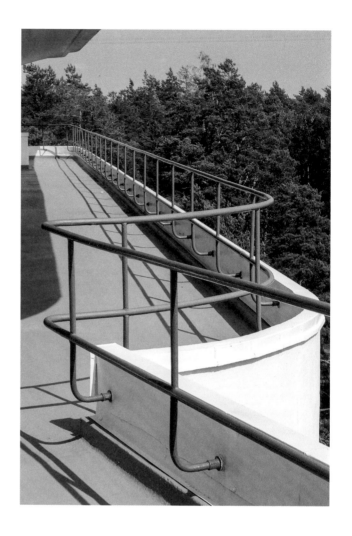

Tuberculosis Sanatorium
Paimio, Finland
1929–1933

Town Hall
Säynätsalo, Finland
1949–1952

Lohiluoma Residential Building
Kauttua, Finland
1942

Terrace Housing
Kauttua, Finland
1937–1938

Architect's House
Helsinki, Finland
1935–1936

Villa Mairea
Noormarkku, Finland
1937–1939

Villa Kokkonen
Järvenpää, Finland
1967–1969

Maison Louis Carré
Bazoches-sur-Guyonne, France
1956–1959, 1961–1963

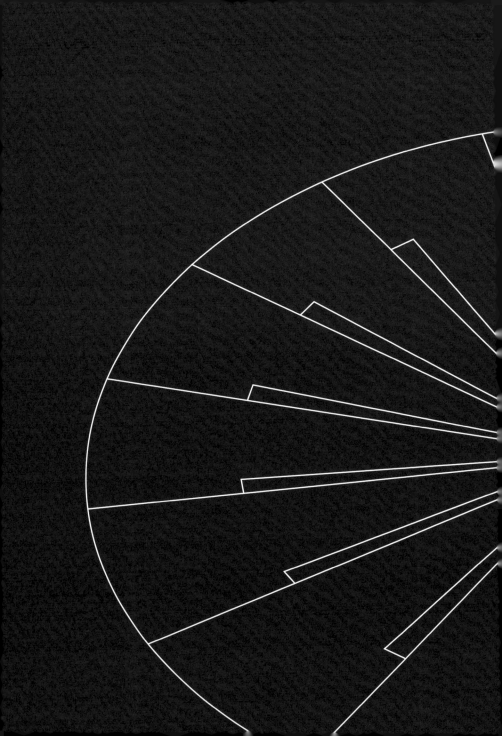

Drainage

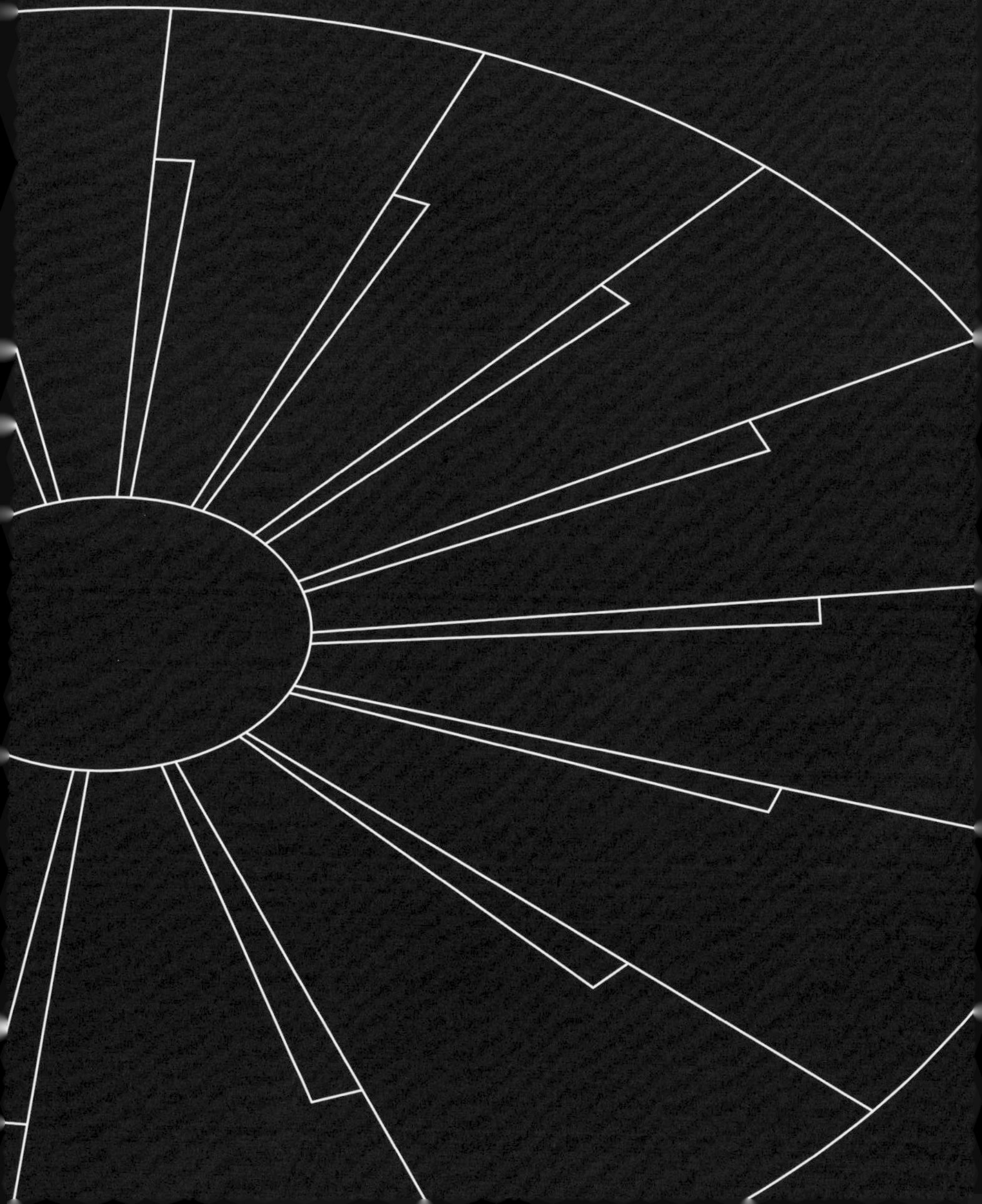

Town Hall
Seinäjoki, Finland
1958–1960

Summer House
Muuratsalo, Finland
1952–1954

Maison Louis Carré
Bazoches-sur-Guyonne, France
1956–1959, 1961–1963

Villa Mairea
Noormarkku, Finland
1937–1939

Maison Louis Carré
Bazoches-sur-Guyonne, France
1956–1959, 1961–1963

Maison Louis Carré
Bazoches-sur-Guyonne, France
1956–1959, 1961–1963

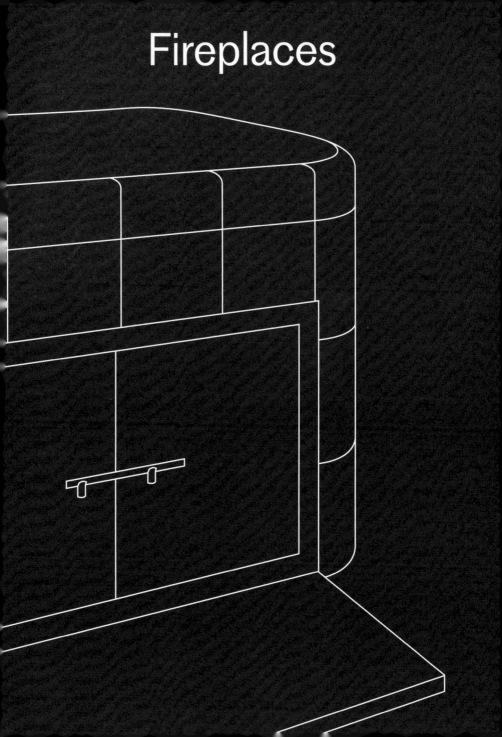

Fireplaces

Architect's House
Helsinki, Finland
1935–1936

Architect's House
Helsinki, Finland
1935–1936

Student Union Building
Jyväskylä, Finland
1961–1964

Student Union Building
Jyväskylä, Finland
1961–1964

Summer House
Muuratsalo, Finland
1952–1954

Summer House
Muuratsalo, Finland
1952–1954

Villa Mairea
Noormarkku, Finland
1937–1939

Tuberculosis Sanatorium
Paimio, Finland
1929–1933

Maison Louis Carré
Bazoches-sur-Guyonne, France
1956–1959, 1961–1963

Maison Louis Carré
Bazoches-sur-Guyonne, France
1956–1959, 1961–1963

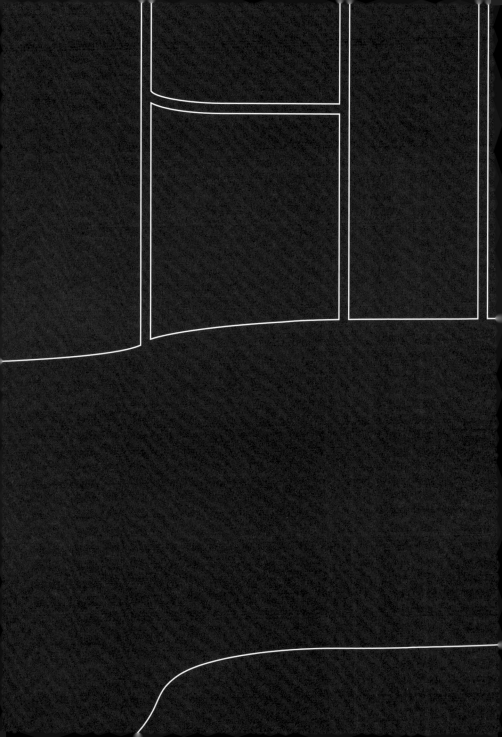

Fixtures

Faculty of Sport and Health
Jyväskylä, Finland
1971

Tuberculosis Sanatorium
Paimio, Finland
1929–1933

Cultural Centre
Helsinki, Finland
1952–1958

University of Jyväskylä Main Building
Jyväskylä, Finland
1954–1956

Alvar Aalto Museum
Jyväskylä, Finland
1971–1973

Tuberculosis Sanatorium
Paimio, Finland
1929–1933

Alvar Aalto Museum
Jyväskylä, Finland
1971–1973

University of Jyväskylä Main Building
Jyväskylä, Finland
1954–1956

Tuberculosis Sanatorium
Paimio, Finland
1929–1933

Tuberculosis Sanatorium
Paimio, Finland
1929–1933

Maison Louis Carré
Bazoches-sur-Guyonne, France
1956–1959, 1961–1963

Architect's House
Helsinki, Finland
1935–1936

Terrace Housing
Kauttua, Finland
1937–1938

Maison Louis Carré
Bazoches-sur-Guyonne, France
1956–1959, 1961–1963

Architect's Studio
Helsinki, Finland
1954–1955, 1962–1963

Architect's Studio
Helsinki, Finland
1954–1955, 1962–1963

Town Hall
Säynätsalo, Finland
1949–1952

Church
Seinäjoki, Finland
1951–1960

Church
Lahti, Finland
1969–1979

Church
Seinäjoki, Finland
1951–1960

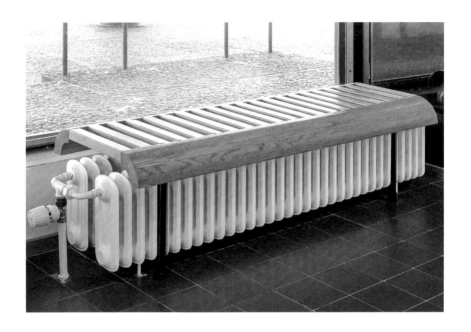

Town Hall
Seinäjoki, Finland
1958–1960

Town Hall
Säynätsalo, Finland
1949–1952

Library
Seinäjoki, Finland
1960–1965

437

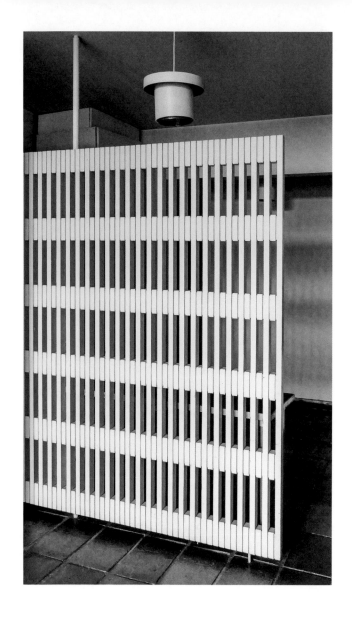

Church
Seinäjoki, Finland
1951–1960

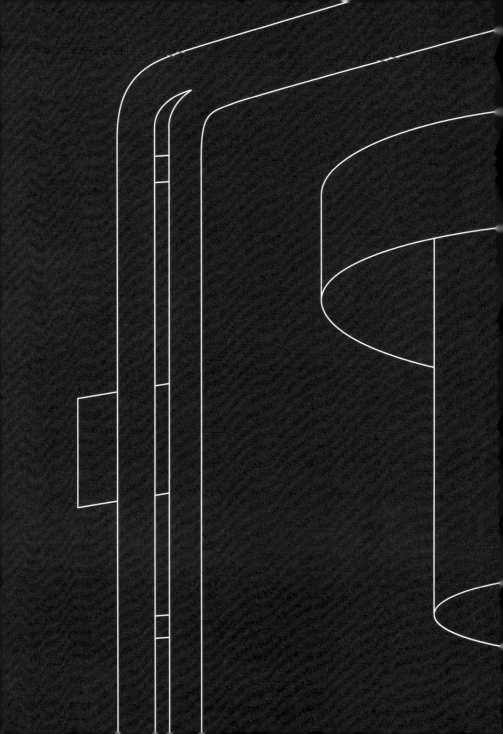

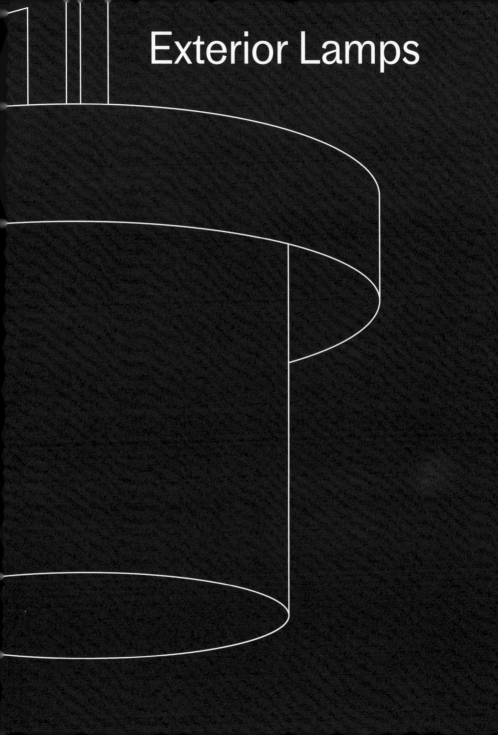

Exterior Lamps

Theatre
Seinäjoki, Finland
1961–1987

Villa Mairea
Noormarkku, Finland
1937–1939

Concert and Convention Hall
Helsinki, Finland
1967–1975

Villa Mairea
Noormarkku, Finland
1937–1939

Enso Gutzeit Housing
Hamina, Finland
1951–1953, 1970–1972

Main Building of the Institute of Technology
Espoo, Finland
1955–1964

Villa Kokkonen
Järvenpää, Finland
1967–1969

Villa Mairea
Noormarkku, Finland
1937–1939

Concert and Convention Hall
Helsinki, Finland
1967–1975

Church
Lahti, Finland
1969–1979

Architect's Studio
Helsinki, Finland
1954–1955, 1962–1963

Cultural Centre
Helsinki, Finland
1952–1958

Public Pensions Institute
Helsinki, Finland
1953–1956

Church
Seinäjoki, Finland
1951–1960

University of Jyväskylä Main Building
Jyväskylä, Finland
1954–1956

Cultural Centre
Helsinki, Finland
1952–1958

Academic Bookshop
Helsinki, Finland
1961–1969

Cultural Centre
Helsinki, Finland
1952–1958

Town Hall
Säynätsalo, Finland
1949–1952

Theatre
Seinäjoki, Finland
1961–1987

Annette Helle
Born and raised in Oslo, Annette Helle is a graduate of ETH Zurich
and TU Delft. She lives in Zurich, where she has run the office of Helle
Architektur since 2001. She has held the position of professor for
design and construction in the Architecture Institute of FHNW Muttenz
since 2010, and she has institute director since 2019.

Céline Dietziker
After training as a draftsperson, Céline Dietziker received her degrees
from FHNW Muttenz and the École Nationale Supérieure d'Architecture
de Paris-Belleville. She has worked in numerous architecture offices
in Basel. Currently, she is an editor at Architektur Basel and a trustee at
the Architektur Dialoge Basel Foundation. Together with Lukas Gruntz,
she has run the office of Atelier Atlas Architektur in Basel since 2021.

Lukas Gruntz
Lukas Gruntz is a graduate of FHNW in Muttenz and Basel, as well as
of the École Nationale Supérieure d'Architecture de Paris-Belleville.
He has worked in architecture offices in Basel, Zurich, and Tokyo. An
editor at Architektur Basel, he is also a regular contributor to various
architectural journals. Together with Céline Dietziker, he has run the
office of Atelier Atlas Architektur in Basel since 2021.

We would like to thank everyone who was involved with this book project, especially Annette Helle for her factual, conceptual, and inspirational support, as well as her insightful text, which contextualized our research. Alexander Felix and Katharina Kulke deserve our gratitude for the stimulating, productive collaboration; they made it possible for the book to appear in this form. We also thank Philipp Möckli and Adrian Schnegg for their fantastic graphic design, which provided the ideal framework for the content. We would especially like to thank Anita Hede and Bruno Trinkler for their generous support. In addition, we are grateful to all the people we met in Finland while visiting the Aaltos' buildings.

With the kind support of
artek

Picture Credit
Alvar Aalto Foundation: p. 8, 9 (Photo: Gustaf Welin), 10, 11 top
(Photo: Eino Mäkinen), 11 bottom (Photo: Hoikkl Havas), 12 bottom
(Photo: Gustaf Welin), 13 (Photo: Martti Kapanen), 14 (Photo: Artek
Collection/Alvar Aalto Foundation), 15 (Photo: propably Christian
Leclerc), 16 (Photo: Kolmio, Artek Collection/Alvar Aalto Foundation)
The Museum of Central Finland: p. 12 top (Photo: Valokuvaamo
Päijänne)
Aalto family collection: p. 17
All other photographies are by Céline Dietziker and Lukas Gruntz.

Translation from German into English: David Haney
Copy editing: John Sweet
Project management: Alexander Felix, Katharina Kulke
Production: Heike Strempel
Layout, cover design and typesetting:
Début Début, Philipp Möckli and Adrian Schnegg
Image Editing: LVD Gesellschaft für Datenverarbeitung mbH, Berlin
Printing: Grafisches Centrum Cuno GmbH & Co. KG, Calbe
Paper: 120 g/m² Amber Graphic

Library of Congress Control Number: 2022930843

Bibliographic information published by the German National Library
The German National Library lists this publication in the Deutsche
Nationalbibliografie; detailed bibliographic data are available on the
Internet at http://dnb.dnb.de.

ISBN 978-3-0356-2332-1
e-ISBN (PDF) 978-3-0356-2334-5
German Print-ISBN 978-3-0356-2331-4

© 2022 Birkhäuser Verlag GmbH, Basel
P.O. Box 44, 4009 Basel, Switzerland
Part of Walter de Gruyter GmbH, Berlin/Boston

9 8 7 6 5 4 3   www.birkhauser.com